A WOMAN'S PLACE

KATELYN BEATY

Participant Guide
by Maria Mayo

Abingdon Press / Nashville

A Woman's Place
A Bible Study Exploring Every Woman's Call to Work
Participant Guide

Copyright © 2017 Abingdon Press
All rights reserved.

This book is printed on elemental chlorine-free paper.
978-1-5018-4900-8

17 18 19 20 21 22 23 24 25 26 — 10 9 8 7 6 5 4 3 2 1
MANUFACTURED IN THE UNITED STATES OF AMERICA

CONTENTS

INTRODUCTION

When it comes to women and work, there is often an "us-versus-them" mentality, dividing women according to the choices they make. Yet, all women have a shared calling to work in a way that glorifies God—whether it be in the office, home, ministry, or beyond. This study gives you the opportunity to gather in conversation around the topic as you explore God's call to work in all its various forms.

How much does the Bible say about women and work? Would you be surprised to know that the answer is *a lot*? In A *Woman's Place*, Katelyn Beaty explores the meaning and value of work for women—work as a way to glorify God—both inside and outside the home. In this study based on Katelyn's book, we ask questions about what the Bible says about women and work and find that the answers may be as beautiful as they are unexpected.

We begin with the contention that women—just like men—are made to reign. We learn that work is holy and good, and that God is the supreme worker in whose image we are all created. God did not make an accident when he made us female, and in Christ we may look forward to a time when gender differences hold no power. We learn about the tangled relationship between work and motherhood, and the integration of work and family. If women are called to work, how can they overcome so many obstacles? Even a single life can bear fruit and a family tree can grow in the new family that Jesus ordains. Finally, we learn that ambition can also be holy, and the "cross-shaped ambition" of Jesus may be what we are all called to emulate.

We engage Scripture to take a deeper dive into these issues. The call to rule in Psalm 8 echoes the Creation story in Genesis 1 and demonstrates how men and women are both—equally—created to work. The words of Paul describe our spiritual gifts and the importance of honoring different gifts. The woman of Proverbs 31 is a model of work and accomplishment. The parable of the Pharisee and the tax collector serves as a potent reminder for women not to judge one another's parenting choices as they decide whether to work outside the home and rather approach each other with humility and grace. Isaiah's verses celebrating barren and single women join Jesus' new definition of family to affirm single women and ensure them a place in the Kingdom. And Katelyn boldly claims that Jesus was the most ambitious person ever to walk the earth. Work is meaningful, and necessary, for all women. Work is one way to glorify God and make meaning out of our lives. According to the Creation story in Genesis 1, it is the very first way.

For each week of our study there are three readings and two sets of questions. Each chapter of the study includes the following elements:

Explore the Message	*A summary of the chapter in the* A Woman's Place *book.*
Read the Scripture	*Selected Scripture passages for the week.*
Ask the Questions	*Questions relating to the Scripture and chapter summary.*
Apply God's Word	*An exploration of the Scripture through the lens of the chapter.*
Think It Through	*Questions to help you think further about the interpretation of Scripture and apply it to your life.*
Bring It Home	*A prompt to think about how the issues affect you personally.*

Write It Down   An *excerpt from* A Woman's Place *and prompts for journaling.*

Pray About It   A *sample prayer to guide you into a personal time of prayer.*

When you plan your study, be sure to allow time to read the corresponding chapter in A *Woman's Place.* This will help you more deeply understand and reflect on the material in this participant guide.

Once a week, you will gather with your group to watch a video in which Katelyn shares additional insights into the material, along with personal stories about her own experience as a working woman. This will also be an opportunity to discuss what you're learning and share how God is working in your life.

As you begin this exploration of women and work, keep your mind and heart open to all the ways Scripture and culture create opportunities for meaningful work for women. All human beings are created to work, and women must not be excluded from that story. Follow Katelyn as she journeys through history and Scripture to discover how women and men alike are called to work that glorifies God.

Session 1
MADE TO REIGN

Session 1

MADE TO REIGN

Explore the Message

"Every human being is made to work," Katelyn Beaty writes in her opening lines. "And since women are human beings, every woman is made to work." We all work, but exactly why is work such an important part of being human? Katelyn looks to Psalm 8 for the answer. The bottom line? We are made to reign over God's creation. Human beings work in order to live into that purpose and bear the image of God on earth. Our God is a God who works, and work is how men and women both properly bear the image of God. What that work looks like runs the full spectrum of human experience, from closing deals in the corner office to making discoveries in the laboratory to caring for children in the home. There are so many possibilities for our work and so many ways we can bear the image of God as we are productive in the world.

The division between men's work and the work that women do has long been prevalent in our culture. Who hasn't heard the saying, "A woman's place is in the home"? But when God created maleness and femaleness, he declared that they were good, and he instructed both of them to rule over creation (Genesis 1:27-31). And this is *why* women are called to work: men can't rule over creation alone. Just for a second, imagine a world in which *only* men did any kind of work. What an incomplete creation! This is not what God intended when he designed men and women. Indeed, "God blessed *them* and said to *them*, 'Be fertile and multiply; fill the earth and master it'" (Genesis 1:28, *emphasis added*). Reigning over all creation is definitely a job for two people.

But what happens when your church tells you that you shouldn't work? Or that your work in the home isn't really work at all? The sad thing is that many Christian communities aren't talking about work at all, much less the work that women do. And some of them are talking about it in ways that are destructive and unbiblical, because it is clear throughout Scripture that women are called to work. Others lack the understanding and resources to engage women who work outside the home, and there are even some that do not adequately affirm those who choose to stay home to raise children and pursue domestic work. As a result, women often find themselves alienated from the very church communities where they should be able to turn for support.

Read the Scripture

¹O Lᴏʀᴅ, *our Lord,*
    how majestic is your name in all the earth!

You have set your glory
    above the heavens.
²*From the lips of children and infants*
    you have ordained praise
because of your enemies,
    to silence the foe and the avenger.

³*When I consider your heavens,*
    the work of your fingers,
the moon and the stars,
    which you have set in place,
⁴*what is man that you are mindful of him,*
    the son of man that you care for him?
⁵*You made him a little lower than the heavenly beings*
    and crowned him with glory and honor.

⁶You made him ruler over the works of your hands;
   you put everything under his feet:
⁷all flocks and herds,
   and the beasts of the field,
⁸the birds of the air,
   and the fish of the sea,
   all that swim the paths of the seas.

⁹O LORD, *our Lord,*
   how majestic is your name in all the earth!

Psalm 8 (NIV 1984)

Ask the Questions

1. Read Psalm 8 out loud. Following Beaty's example, in verses 3-6, substitute your own name for "him" or "his." How does it feel? Can you imagine yourself as the object of God's particular attention and care? What do you rule over in your daily life?
2. Do you find it difficult to read the psalm as directed at both men and women? If so, why?
3. Summarize what the psalmist is saying in verse 4. How do these words make you feel about your role in God's creation?

Apply God's Word

"O LORD, our Lord, / how majestic is your name in all the earth!" What a triumphant beginning to the very first song of praise that appears in the Book of Psalms. The psalm is unique in that it addresses God directly: "You have set your glory above the heavens," and "You put everything under his feet." The words of this song of celebration raise up both God's power over the world and the important role and work of human beings. Just think of the job God gave us, to rule over *everything*! "Psalm 8 is first and foremost about God," writes Katelyn. "But it is also about humankind: *their* majesty, glory, and power, a reflection of the God whose image they bear." We are created in the image of the amazing God described in Psalm 8. What a cause for thanks and praise!

But what does this psalm have to do with work? Take a look at Genesis 1:26-28:

> ²⁶Then God said, "Let us make humanity in our image to resemble us so that they may take charge of the fish of the sea, the birds in the sky, the livestock, all the earth, and all the crawling things on earth."
>
> ²⁷God created humanity in God's own image,
> in the divine image God created them,
> male and female God created them.
>
> ²⁸God blessed them and said to them, "Be fertile and multiply; fill the earth and master it. Take charge of the fish of the sea, the birds in the sky, and everything crawling on the ground."
>
> (Genesis 1:26-28)

Sound familiar? Psalm 8 repeats the Genesis themes: "You made him ruler over the works of your hands; / you put everything under his feet," all the birds and animals and fish in the sea. We were made to rule. And, more importantly, we were made to *work*.

Throughout Scripture, God is described as working. Bear with me for some quick Hebrew so we can look more closely at that idea. When you see the noun "work" in the Genesis account of creation, the Hebrew word is *melakah*. This word means work, business, or occupation. Genesis 2:2 describes, "On the sixth day, God completed all the work [*melakah*] that he had done." God worked to make all of creation, and on the seventh day, he rested. This is just as we are instructed to do in the Ten Commandments: "Six days you may work and do all your tasks [*melakah*], but the seventh day is a Sabbath" (Exodus 20:9-10). The psalm reminds us of this God who works and how we are created in his image, also to work. Katelyn writes, "Psalm 8 helps us to remember a bedrock truth about *why* we work. We work in order to live into God's purposes for all of us: to reign over all of creation as his image bearers and representatives on earth."

Remember that in Genesis 1, both men and women are created to rule over God's creation. Don't be fooled by the "him" language in the psalm; this term, along with "Son of Man," is meant to refer to all of humanity, men and women together. And just as "him" refers to all of

We can realize that
we are not isolated in
our work dreams,
that we are not alone
in our deepest desires
to make our professions live
again and be true to
their deepest moral and
spiritual potentials. The word
community, after all,
means "to work on a
common task together."[1]

---

1. Matthew Fox, *The Reinvention of Work: A New Vision of Livelihood for Our Time* (New York: HarperCollins, 1994), 135.

us, it also refers to each of us. No doubt, to be created in the image of God is to be overflowing with glory and honor. The psalm's celebration of our humanity speaks to all of us about the work we are invited to do for the glory of God.

Reading this psalm alongside the Genesis account paints a graceful picture of how we live out our call as God's image bearers and how work is an integral part of that. It is clear that men's work and the work of women are equally created and equally valued in God's creation. He created all of us together, and we work to reflect his image. When Christian communities neglect the fullness of the Psalm 8 celebration, creation fails to flourish. God created a world that was complete only when women and men worked side by side to care for it. The psalm remembers and celebrates this. Women, like men, are only slightly less than divine (v. 5). With everything under our feet (v. 6), we are made to work and made to reign.

Think It Through

1. Read Genesis 1:26-28 above. How does the voice of Genesis come through in Psalm 8? In what ways is the Creation story affirmed and celebrated?
2. Consider the idea that all women are called to work. What does that mean for your life?
3. Katelyn makes the point that work is a crucial part of bearing the image of God. Name several ways that this is true in your experience.
4. Do you feel that your church community is supportive of the work you do? Why or why not?
5. Think about your own work. In what ways does it reflect the image of God?

Bring It Home

Write down a list of some of the women you know. Beside each of their names, list the ways that they work—at home, at church, in the wider world. Do you find that your community values the various kinds of work they do? If so, how does that manifest?

Write It Down

Read the following excerpt from A *Woman's Place*. Choose one (or both) of the questions and write a response in a journal or notebook.

"For women to live on mission, we Christians need to massively rethink how we think and talk about work. In both subtle and not so subtle ways, Christian women are being discouraged from thinking of work as a good, direct way of bearing the image of God and living on mission for him."

1. What do you think it means "to live on mission"? In what ways do you live on mission for God in your life? What keeps you from doing so?
2. What does work mean to you? How is your work related to your faith? Do you feel called to the work you do?

Pray About It

Oh God, let me be a true bearer of your image on the earth. Let the work of my hands please you and delight you. Inspire me in my work and make me fruitful and productive. Grant me the wisdom to make sound choices and care for your creation as I move through my day. I thank you for the gifts you have given me and the world you have placed under my feet. Amen.

Session 2

WHY "LEANING IN" IS GOOD— AND NOT ENOUGH

Session 2

WHY "LEANING IN" IS GOOD— AND NOT ENOUGH

Explore the Message

In 2013, Sheryl Sandberg, the chief operating officer of Facebook, wrote a book called *Lean In: Women, Work, and the Will to Lead*, which created quite a buzz—both positive and negative. In it, she explores why women occupy so few leadership positions in government and industry. She encourages women to take their rightful places at the table and offers practical advice for negotiating, finding a mentor, setting boundaries, and building a satisfying career. At no point does Sandberg denigrate work inside the home. Rather, she seems to hope that women who love their work outside the home will not abandon it because they think they can't have a family as well.

While *Lean In* discusses the "how" of work, it falls short of addressing the big question of "why" we work, wherever our "workplace" might be. And the answer is not that we are on a quest for a promotion or a corner office, as much of Sandberg's advice might seem to suggest. Katelyn Beaty points out that much of what Sandberg proposes requires a position of privilege as a starting point. Asking for a raise, leading meetings, navigating your company's leave policy, or hiring a nanny all assume a particular place in life. Yet many of us are not in the position to make such choices about work. And not everyone assumes that personal success is the point of work in the first place. You may not desire to be the COO of anything, and that certainly doesn't mean your work lacks meaning. So why do we work?

The answer may not be the same for women as it is for men, and Beaty points out that the larger cultural conversation about work simply takes the ways that men work and applies that to women. But God offers a diversity of gifts, and a diversity in how and why we work. Some churches discourage women from pursuing professional success, subtly implying that you can't work outside the home *and* have a family while doing either one very well. But that doesn't have to be the only Christian response. Instead, writes Katelyn, "The Christian response is to recover the holy, human, world-altering, and self-giving purposes of work itself." Whatever kind of work you do, you can find this Christian response. All kinds of work and any kind of spiritual gift can be holy, human, world-altering, and self-giving.

Read the Scripture

5Though there are many of us, we are one body in Christ, and individually we belong to each other. 6We have different gifts that are consistent with God's grace that has been given to us. If your gift is prophecy, you should prophesy in proportion to your faith. 7If your gift is service, devote yourself to serving. If your gift is teaching, devote yourself to teaching. 8If your gift is encouragement, devote yourself to encouraging. The one giving should do it with no strings attached. The leader should lead with passion. The one showing mercy should be cheerful.

9Love should be shown without pretending. Hate evil, and hold on to what is good. 10Love each other like the members of your family. Be the best at showing honor to each other.

Romans 12:5-10

[4]There are different spiritual gifts but the same Spirit; [5]and there are different ministries and the same Lord; [6]and there are different activities but the same God who produces all of them in everyone. [7]A demonstration of the Spirit is given to each person for the common good. [8]A word of wisdom is given by the Spirit to one person, a word of knowledge to another according to the same Spirit, [9]faith to still another by the same Spirit, gifts of healing to another in the one Spirit, [10]performance of miracles to another, prophecy to another, the ability to tell spirits apart to another, different kinds of tongues to another, and the interpretation of the tongues to another. [11]All these things are produced by the one and same Spirit who gives what he wants to each person.

1 Corinthians 12:4-11

Ask the Questions

1. Read Romans 12:5-10 and 1 Corinthians 12:4-11 out loud. What is each of these passages saying about diversity in work among God's people? What gifts resonate with you?
2. Imagine that Romans 12:5-10 and 1 Corinthians 12:4-11 are Paul's response to a question that someone asked him. What would that question be?

Apply God's Word

What is your gift? According to Romans, each of us has at least one gift. And according to First Corinthians, each person receives a gift of the Spirit for the common good. Some are teachers, some are prophets; others are encouraging, and still others are compassionate. There is a vast diversity in all the spiritual gifts, but all come from the one God who bestows them on everyone. Our only charge is to do the best we can with the gift(s) we receive. If our gift is serving, we should devote ourselves to serving. We should lead with passion. We should mother with care and good humor. We should write with dedication and concentration. Whatever our work is, we should do it with the most skill and energy possible. Look around you. What is the evidence of your spiritual gift(s)? Do you sit in an office with books and pages of research? Are you at home with children to care for? How can we be sure that we are making the most of our own spiritual gifts?

I do not believe that there is one
definition of success or happiness.
Not all women want careers.
Not all women want children.
Not all women want both.
I would never advocate that we
should all have the same objectives.
Many people are not interested in
acquiring power, not because they
lack ambition, but because they are
living their lives as they desire.
Some of the most important
contributions to our world are
made by caring for one person
at a time. We each have to
chart our own unique course
and define which goals fit our
lives, values, and dreams.[1]

---

1.   Sheryl Sandberg, *Lean In: Women, Work, and the Will to Lead* (New York: Alfred A. Knopf, 2013), 10

In Romans, Paul lists seven spiritual gifts, a number that indicates wholeness. In this case, the number seven is representative of the full list of spiritual gifts that could be given; that is, here are seven possible gifts, but the real number of gifts is endless. As 1 Corinthians 12 clarifies, every single person has a spiritual gift; the Greek word *hekastos* means "each one individually" (v. 7). Take a moment and let that sink in. God looked specifically at *you* and chose a spiritual gift for *you* alone.

The emphasis on difference is so important to Paul that he repeats it three times at the beginning of the First Corinthians passage: different gifts, but the same spirit; different ministries and the same Lord; different activities but the same God. Nowhere does the text indicate that men and women have different vocations, only that *each individual person* has a different spiritual gift. Look for a minute at the phrase in verse 6: "different activities but the same God." In the original Greek, what is translated here as "different activities" is *diaireseis energematon*, or, literally, different work. *Energematon* is a general term in Greek that encompasses all manner of work. What this verse is getting at is that God gives each of us work to do, and we are charged with doing the best work we can.

In the Romans passage, Paul emphasizes that all members of the Christian community should strive for unity. In other words, our separate gifts do not compete with one another, and neither is one vocation better than the other. On the contrary, each of our gifts contributes perfectly to the whole body of Christ. He writes, "Individually we belong to each other" (v. 5). Think about that. As individuals, we all belong to each other in the body of Christ. The gifts and work of men and women are equally valuable, just as each part of the human body is separate and valuable and necessary to the whole. As he points out in 1 Corinthians 12, "The eye can't say to the hand, 'I don't need you,' or in turn, the head can't say to the feet, 'I don't need you'" (v. 21). We can't say to one another "I don't need you" just because our vocations are different. What kind of world would we have without teachers, executives, mothers, or architects? Who are we to say that one of those careers is more valuable than the other? Instead, as Paul would say, whatever work you do, be the best at it.

And not only that, but we are to respect everyone else and the work they do as well. In a world that is focused on acquiring honor for the self, Paul shifts the lens. "Love each other like the members of your family," he writes. "Be the best at showing honor to each other" (Romans 12:10). This is part of the goal of unity. This is what the body of Christ looks like on earth: each of us doing our own work with the great variety of gifts that God has given us, and all of us showing honor to one another the best we possibly can. In response to the challenges for women in their work outside the home, Katelyn writes, "I am grateful that God delights in giving his people a diversity of gifts and calls us to 'outdo one another in showing honor,' seeing and naming each other's unique contributions."

Think It Through

1. Think about your own spiritual gift(s). Remember that you may have more than one. What are they? If you're not sure, what gifts have others affirmed in you?
2. Does understanding the way that spiritual gifts are given to the body of Christ change the way you think about work? If so, how and why?
3. One of Katelyn's critiques of *Lean In* is that it discusses the "how" of work, but not the "why" of work. She discusses this more in the chapters to follow. Based on what you know so far, what would you say is the "why" of work, especially for women? What does Scripture say about this?
4. How are spiritual gifts related to work? How do you put your own spiritual gift(s) to use in the work you do?
5. Does Paul's metaphor of the human body give you clarity about your own role in using your gifts in your work? How does this metaphor speak to unity in the body of Christ, and where might it fall short?

Bring It Home

Think about the members of your family. What spiritual gifts would you say each of them has? Remember, there are more spiritual gifts than just what Paul mentions, so you can think of gifts that aren't on his list. Does each person's gift correspond with his or her work? Make a list of all the gifts you can identify. Are you surprised at what you find?

Write It Down

Read the following excerpt from A Woman's Place. Choose one (or both) of the questions and write a response in a journal or notebook.

"Most of us have inherited a flawed view of why women or men work [outside the home] at all. According to the mainstream secular narrative in the West, work is fundamentally about what it can give *you* rather than what you can give it. What it seemingly can give you is security, in the form of ever growing paychecks and an ample retirement nest egg; or affirmation, in the form of outranking colleagues or growing your Twitter following or gleaning awards or invites to exclusive events; or power, in the form of shaping a corporate culture and having others know how important you are. To be sure, security, affirmation, and power are not inherently bad. But they become bad—that is, idols—when we try to wrest them from our work rather than resting in God's perfect provision of all three."

1. In your own experience, does work provide you with security, affirmation, and power? In what ways?
2. What do *you* bring to your work? How is your work an expression of your spiritual gifts? How does your work bring honor to others and contribute to the unity of the body of Christ?

Pray About It

Dear God, thank you for helping me to think about my complex world of work. I am grateful to be reminded of my intentional spiritual gifts and my particular place in the perfect and whole body of Christ. May I be mindful of honoring others as I work and always remember that work is not for me, but for you. Amen.

Session 3

OUR GENEROUS WORKER GOD

Session 3

OUR GENEROUS WORKER GOD

Explore the Message

Have you ever thought of God as a worker? The first thing God does in Scripture is work: "In the beginning God *created*" (Genesis 1:1 NIV, *emphasis added*). God created male and female *together* to bear his image and work in the world he created. Just as Adam and Eve needed one another's work in the garden, so do all human beings rely on the work of others for food, clothing, and other material items. Katelyn Beaty observes that we all need work, women and men alike, to thrive in the world. In fact, she writes, "Work...is a fundamental way to preserve the dignity of all people." This holds true whether we stay at home with kids or work outside the home. Work brings dignity to all of us.

Work is not just what we do for a paycheck, but, as it was for Adam and Eve, work is how we interact with the world for our sustenance and benefit. Some of the hardest work in the world happens in the home, without pay or promotion or sometimes even praise. Some of the most joyous, fulfilling work happens there, too, like gathering friends together and serving them a meal. Work happens in community. "We were never meant to work just for ourselves or just for our families,"

Katelyn writes. "We were meant to work so that flourishing, wholeness, and delight would spread to the furthest reaches of creation." This is the meaning of *shalom* that is missing in many understandings of work, especially those that confine the work of women to the home or assume that all women want to climb the corporate ladder.

Work is also an opportunity to serve. Women who are pursuing *shalom* in whatever varieties of work are acting as the *tsaddiqim*, Hebrew for "righteous." This is what shapes the meaning of work in a way that discussions that only address the "how" of work don't quite get to. To live as the *tsaddiqim*, Katelyn writes, "means...that work is a core way we honor God, serve others, and remember that our allegiance to Christ and his kingdom trumps our other allegiances and roles." This means living out righteousness and *shalom* in the world, both men and women, regardless of what outdated stereotypes say that we are meant to do. We can all do the work of the *tsaddiqim*, and this is the kind of work we are created to do. Any work can take on a spiritual, righteous dimension if we let it. Find your ministry where you are and live into it fully.

Read the Scripture

²⁶*Then God said, "Let us make humanity in our image to resemble us so that they may take charge of the fish of the sea, the birds in the sky, the livestock, all the earth, and all the crawling things on earth."*

> ²⁷*God created humanity in God's own image,*
> *in the divine image God created them,*
> *male and female God created them.*

²⁸*God blessed them and said to them, "Be fertile and multiply; fill the earth and master it. Take charge of the fish of the sea, the birds in the sky, and everything crawling on the ground." ²⁹Then God said, "I now give to you all the plants on the earth that yield seeds and all the trees whose fruit produces its seeds within it. These will be your food. ³⁰To all wildlife, to all the birds in the sky, and to everything crawling on the ground—to everything that breathes—I give all the green grasses for food." And that's*

what happened. [31]God saw everything he had made: it was supremely good.

There was evening and there was morning: the sixth day.

Genesis 1:26-31

[18]Then the LORD God said, "It's not good that the human is alone. I will make him a helper that is perfect for him." [19]So the LORD God formed from the fertile land all the wild animals and all the birds in the sky and brought them to the human to see what he would name them. The human gave each living being its name. [20]The human named all the livestock, all the birds in the sky, and all the wild animals. But a helper perfect for him was nowhere to be found.

[21]So the LORD God put the human into a deep and heavy sleep, and took one of his ribs and closed up the flesh over it. [22]With the rib taken from the human, the LORD God fashioned a woman and brought her to the human being. [23]The human said,

> "This one finally is bone from my bones
>   and flesh from my flesh.
> She will be called a woman
>   because from a man she was taken."

[24]This is the reason that a man leaves his father and mother and embraces his wife, and they become one flesh.

Genesis 2:18-24

Ask the Questions

1. What does it mean to think of God as a worker? How does God work today?
2. Think about how you learned the Creation story as a child. What details stuck out to you? Were you taught that Eve was inferior to Adam, or that Adam was the more important one?
3. "Be fertile and multiply; fill the earth and master it" (Genesis 1:28). This is perhaps the first description of the work of human beings. In what way do these words describe the work we do every day, both in and out of the home?

[16]Let your work be shown to your servants,
and your glorious power to their children.
[17]Let the favor of the Lord our God be upon us,
and establish the work of our hands upon us;
yes, establish the work of our hands!

Psalm 90:16-17 (ESV)

God's *shalom*, peace, involves
inevitable righteousness, justice,
wholesomeness, fullness of life,
participation in decision
making, goodness, laughter,
joy, compassion, sharing,
and reconciliation.[1]

---

1. Desmond Tutu, selected and introduced by Naomi Tutu, *The Words of Desmond Tutu* (New York: Newmarket Press, 1989), 47.

Apply God's Word

For six days, God works to create everything we know in the world. He creates the light and the dark, the dome and the waters, the earth and the sea. God creates all the plants and living creatures, and then he comes to his crowning achievement: human beings, male and female. And because he creates them in his image, the human beings are also created to work. Male and female reflect God's image *together*, and they do so by working. They are appointed to tend and take care of the world that God has created.

In the second version of the Creation story, God looks at the one human being and declares that he should not be alone. He seeks to find a "helper perfect for him" and first has the man consider each of the animals. With no luck there, God creates a woman out of the man's rib, and she is the ideal partner. Thus Adam and Eve are created, and their match is perfect. But don't get the idea that Eve is somehow inferior to Adam. The literal translation of the Hebrew *ezer kenegdo*—here translated as "helper perfect for him"—is counterpart, or corresponding partner. Even coworker. Certainly not assistant. The word is used throughout the Old Testament to refer to God, who himself is quite a powerful partner in times of need. Read Exodus 18:4, for example: "The God of my ancestors was my helper who rescued me from Pharaoh's sword." Or Deuteronomy 33:26: "No one compares to God! / He rides through heaven to help you." Here, God is defined with the same word, *ezer*. Imagine that Eve is this kind of helper, an equal partner in strength and protection.

There is nothing subordinate about an *ezer kenegdo*. "One flesh," reads the Scripture (Genesis 2:24). Equals. Together they are to work and care for the creation. What they got into along the way is a whole other story, but even after they ate from the tree, they were charged to work together in the world. Like all human beings, Adam and Eve *needed* their work. And God had big expectations for them. They should work to create more human beings, of course, but they should also work to continue the creation of the world itself. Katelyn writes, "The buildings, food, laws, courts, gardens, clothes, calendars, dances, languages, and the million other artifacts and ideas that comprise culture are what

35

God anticipates as he invites his image bearers to take up the creative task." That's a lot of work to accomplish. Look around you: all the books and stores and farms and cathedrals and every other detail in the world are the work of human hands, laboring in the image of God. Everything you have built in your home is a continuation of what Adam and Eve began as they cared for the world and mastered it. Our work creates our world.

Do you know anyone who has ever lost a job? Along with the fear and anxiety that comes with losing a paycheck, there is also the stress of losing a primary source of identity and meaning. A period of unemployment can be one of the most trying times a person can experience. We need work to make our time meaningful (there's a reason God only gave us one day to rest), to support our families by earning money or providing care, and to serve others as the righteous in the world. This applies to all kinds of work, not just work outside the home. Without meaningful work, we suffer physically, spiritually, and emotionally. Without work, we struggle to reflect the image of God. From the story of Adam and Eve, we are reassured that work is an essential part of that reflection.

Think It Through

1. Throughout the Old Testament, the word *tsaddiq* is used to mean "righteous." How does this word apply to your daily work? In what ways is your work a way to honor God and serve others?
2. *Ezer kenegdo* has been translated into English in many ways: a helper perfect for him, a suitable helper, aid, suitable companion, helper fit for him, help meet. Which name speaks to you the most, and why? Which do you feel is the most accurate?
3. Katelyn writes, "The good news is that none of us has to become a pastor, a missionary, or even a social justice Christian to live as *tsaddiq* in our sphere of influence." All work is holy, not just that which we label with religious language. How is your own work holy?

4. In what ways does the work you do give your life meaning? If you work outside the home, think about what it would mean for you to lose your job. What would it mean for you, financially, spiritually, and emotionally?

Bring It Home

Think about a child you know. It can be one of your own, or a relative's or friend's child. Imagine that you will tell this child the story of God's creation of human beings without using the Bible or any kind of book. What kind of language would you use? How would you explain the relationship between male and female? What would be the role of work in your story?

Write It Down

Read the following excerpt from A *Woman's Place*. Choose one (or both) of the questions and write a response in a journal or notebook.

"If work is good and dignifying for men; if it is good and dignifying for people in developing countries receiving microloans to start their own businesses; if it is good and dignifying for college graduates landing their first job—then work is good and dignifying for the stay-at-home mother with three kids. We would be remiss not to see that."

1. When you were a child, what was your experience of work in your family? Did you grow up expecting to work outside the home? What is your relationship to work today?
2. What makes work dignifying and good? Think about your experiences with work, both outside the home and inside. What are examples of how work has been meaningful to you? When has it been a source of dignity and goodness?

Pray About It

Thank you, God, for the work of my hands that gives meaning to my everyday life. I feel so blessed to be able to share my talents and to work to be righteous in the world. Please provide opportunities for meaningful and fair work to all of us who thirst for them. I hope the work I do today will bring sustenance and joy to everyone I touch. I labor for your honor and glory. Amen.

Session 4

WOMEN HAVE ALWAYS WORKED

Session 4

WOMEN HAVE ALWAYS WORKED

Explore the Message

What are the role models of working women in your life? Katelyn Beaty points to her very industrious grandmother, who grew their food, made their rugs, cooked elaborate meals, and even managed a greenhouse. She was as productive as the woman described in Proverbs 31, and she worked with the same "willing hands" (Proverbs 31:13 NRSV). Both Katelyn's grandmother, whose work flourished in the home, and the "capable wife" of Proverbs 31 (NRSV), who was engaged in work both in the home and in the community, give support to the idea that women have always worked. The idea that women are morally bound to confine their efforts to the home is relatively recent. Throughout much of history, women have worked inside and outside the home, and the Bible has many examples of women working in various ways.

Some Christian communities teach that women should not work outside the home, or that women who do risk overshadowing and intimidating their partners or neglecting family and domestic responsibilities. But aligning work outside the home solely with men, and domestic tasks solely with women, and then calling that division of roles biblical, confuses what we find in the Bible with what we've heard in our culture. Nowhere in the Bible do we see the suggestion that women should not work. Women were active in the economy of the ancient world. The woman in Proverbs 31 is one example, but don't forget about Mary Magdalene, Joanna, and Susanna—all of whom were women of some means who helped fund Jesus' ministry (Luke 8:1-3). Lydia was a successful businesswoman who worked with Paul (Acts 16:14), and Phoebe, a deacon, was a "benefactor of many" in Paul's ministry (Romans 16:1-2 NRSV). Priscilla worked as a leather-worker alongside Paul and her husband Aquila (Acts 18:2-3).

Throughout modern history, women have continued to work. During and after the Industrial Revolution, the idea of men and women occupying "separate spheres" began to emerge among the middle and upper classes and persists today. In an agrarian society, men and women worked side by side to run a farm or a shop, producing whatever goods would sustain them. In the last few centuries, women have worked in their own homes, other people's homes, and later in factories and stores. As factories took over much of the work of the home, motherhood became a profession in itself, something that could be researched and perfected; and in the ensuing years the "profession of motherhood" has been highly esteemed in many Christian communities. Somehow the idea that women must devote themselves exclusively to the home and to raising children while only men are meant to work outside the home has been integrated back into the Scripture as though God created the world that way. Such an idea, Katelyn writes, "threatens to keep women from knowing the good and holy purposes of work, whether inside the home or outside of it."

What, then, are we to make of Scriptures such as 1 Timothy 5:14, "I want younger widows to marry, have children, and manage their homes," and Titus 2:5, in which women are instructed to be "sensible, morally pure, [and] working at home"? By reading these words with our contemporary notion of what it means to be "in the home," we miss the enormity of the task in the first-century context. Since the home was such an important site of productivity, to manage one's home was actually a position of authority. Home was not the opposite of work, but the setting for it. For much of history, the home was often a primary workplace for women and men alike.

Women have always worked. Throughout history, women have been important contributors not only to their families and communities but also to local economies and places of industry. From biblical times to today, women have worked to bear the image of a creative, working God—wherever that work might take place. Imagine a world where only men work and women are not allowed to work, either outside or inside the home. What contributions would be lost! God created all of us to work in his image.

Read the Scripture

¹⁰A capable wife who can find?
   She is far more precious than jewels.
¹¹The heart of her husband trusts in her,
   and he will have no lack of gain.
¹²She does him good, and not harm,
   all the days of her life.
¹³She seeks wool and flax,
   and works with willing hands.
¹⁴She is like the ships of the merchant,
   she brings her food from far away.
¹⁵She rises while it is still night
   and provides food for her household
   and tasks for her servant-girls.
¹⁶She considers a field and buys it;
   with the fruit of her hands she plants a vineyard.
¹⁷She girds herself with strength,
   and makes her arms strong.
¹⁸She perceives that her merchandise is profitable.
   Her lamp does not go out at night.
¹⁹She puts her hands to the distaff,
   and her hands hold the spindle.
²⁰She opens her hand to the poor,
   and reaches out her hands to the needy.
²¹She is not afraid for her household when it snows,
   for all her household are clothed in crimson.

[22]*She makes herself coverings;*
     her clothing is fine linen and purple.
[23]*Her husband is known in the city gates,*
     taking his seat among the elders of the land.
[24]*She makes linen garments and sells them;*
     she supplies the merchant with sashes.
[25]*Strength and dignity are her clothing,*
     and she laughs at the time to come.
[26]*She opens her mouth with wisdom,*
     and the teaching of kindness is on her tongue.
[27]*She looks well to the ways of her household,*
     and does not eat the bread of idleness.
[28]*Her children rise up and call her happy;*
     her husband too, and he praises her:
[29]*"Many women have done excellently,*
     but you surpass them all."
[30]*Charm is deceitful, and beauty is vain,*
     but a woman who fears the LORD *is to be praised.*
[31]*Give her a share in the fruit of her hands,*
     and let her works praise her in the city gates.

                                        Proverbs 31:10-31 (NRSV)

[1]*Soon afterward, Jesus traveled through the cities and villages, preaching and proclaiming the good news of God's kingdom. The Twelve were with him,* [2]*along with some women who had been healed of evil spirits and sicknesses. Among them were Mary Magdalene (from whom seven demons had been thrown out),* [3]*Joanna (the wife of Herod's servant Chuza), Susanna, and many others who provided for them out of their resources.*

                                        Luke 8:1-3

[1]*After this, Paul left Athens and went to Corinth.* [2]*There he found a Jew named Aquila, a native of Pontus. He had recently come from Italy with his wife Priscilla because Claudius had ordered all Jews to leave Rome. Paul visited with them.* [3]*Because they practiced the same trade, he stayed and worked with them. They all worked with leather.*

                                        Acts 18:1-3

³Say hello to Prisca and Aquila, my coworkers in Christ Jesus, ⁴who risked their own necks for my life. I'm not the only one who thanks God for them, but all the churches of the Gentiles do the same. ⁵Also say hello to the church that meets in their house. Say hello to Epaenetus, my dear friend, who was the first convert in Asia for Christ. ⁶Say hello to Mary, who has worked very hard for you. ⁷Say hello to Andronicus and Junia, my relatives and my fellow prisoners. They are prominent among the apostles, and they were in Christ before me.

Romans 16:3-7

Ask the Questions

1. How often have you heard the Proverbs 31 woman praised for being a good wife? A loving mother? What about a hard worker, or successful businesswoman? Which of her accomplishments stands out to you?
2. Jesus' ministry included women at nearly every turn. Women worked alongside him and sometimes funded his mission. What does this say about the work of women in the first century? Do women play as important a role in your own church community? Why or why not?
3. Katelyn explains that in the New Testament the home was not a place of idleness, but rather a busy center of the economy in the first century. Do you think this is still true? Why or why not?

Apply God's Word

How would you feel if you lived next door to the Proverbs 31 woman? First of all, she stays up all night (v. 18). What a distraction! Everything she says is wise and kind (v. 26). Her husband thinks she is amazing (v. 29). She can make *anything* (vv. 13, 19, 21, 22, 24). Even her *children* sing her praises (v. 28)! What *can't* this woman do? One thing is clear, though. She *works*. She gets things done, both in and out of the house. She's buying fields, selling her goods, importing food, and, most importantly, being praised for it. Clearly she is a woman of many talents and good business sense. As a next-door neighbor she might be a little intimidating. Who wants to compare themselves to someone like that? But joking aside, Proverbs 31 :10-31 is a hymn of praise to *all* women. The first verse of the poem starts with the first letter of the Hebrew alphabet, and then the next verse the second, and on until the end. Verses 10-31 are enclosed by the entire Hebrew alphabet, symbolizing wholeness and thus the praise of all women, everywhere.

To be sure, the Proverbs 31 woman is a beautiful example of working in the image of God. The Hebrew verb *asa* is used to describe God's creation of the world, as when "God made the dome and separated the waters" (Genesis 1:7) and "God made the stars and two great lights" (Genesis 1:16). This word is also applied to the Proverbs 31 woman when "her works praise her" Proverbs 31:31 NRSV). As a reflection of the work of God, who creates even with his fingers (Psalm 8:3), the Proverbs 31 woman is busy with handcrafts—making clothes, spinning wool, dyeing fabric. She "works with willing hands" (v. 13 NRSV), and the same language (Hebrew *asa*) is used to describe "the works of [God's] hands" in Psalm 8:66 (NRSV). Praised by everyone, this woman works and creates and provides for her family just as God intended human beings to do. We don't all do *all* of the things the Proverbs 31 woman does, but these are the kinds of things that women did in her time.

The Proverbs 31 woman takes on all manner of work, and there is no discussion of gender or appropriateness of that work for a woman. The phrase "capable wife" (or "capable woman"; Hebrew *eshet chayil*) is the female counterpart to Scripture's "capable men" (Hebrew *anshe chayil*), ones who are strong and wise and valiant in all kinds of pursuits (see Genesis 47:6 and Exodus 18:21). Clearly, men are not the only ones who can be capable. There are two other "capable women" mentioned in the Old Testament: the good wife of Proverbs 12:4, and Ruth, called so by Boaz in Ruth 3:11. Today, the phrase *eshet chayil*, which also means "woman of valor," is used among Jewish women as a kind of cheer: "You go, girl!" What a wonderful way to use the Proverbs 31 woman to encourage, rather than intimidate or compare.

The Proverbs 31 woman, described in this poem intended for a male audience, may have been intended to correct inaccurate perceptions of women and encourage men to praise them. In any case, here we have

Eshet chayil
is best translated
"valorous woman."
Using this phrasing highlights
the fact that this poem is
a song of praise for
women rather than
a "to do" list.[1]

---

1. Kimberly Dunnam Reisman, *The Christ-Centered Woman: Finding Balance in a World of Extremes* (Nashville: Abingdon Press, 2013), 27.

a generous portrait of a working woman who is praised not only by her family but also "in the city gates" (v. 31), the equivalent of throughout the land. She is productive and charitable and savvy and talented. She is a perfect biblical example of how women have always worked, even if she was a bit of a workaholic.

We see in the New Testament that nearly five centuries after Proverbs 31 sang the praises of the ideal woman, women continued to play a part in the working world both inside and outside the home. Priscilla and Aquila were both leather-workers when they met Paul. Acts 18:3 reads, "Because they practiced the same trade, he stayed and worked with them. They all worked with leather." Later, Paul refers to both of them as his "coworkers in Christ Jesus" (Greek *sunergoi*; Romans 16:3), so technically Priscilla and Aquila are each working two jobs: leather-working and missionary work. Paul doesn't say anything about whether Priscilla *should* be working with her husband in either context. In fact, there are a number of women working in leadership roles alongside Paul. Romans 16:1-7 introduces Phoebe and Mary, and also Junia, who is called "prominent among the apostles" (Romans 16:7). Here again, it is clear: women have always worked.

Women were not only workers for Paul, but they contributed mightily to Jesus' ministry as well. Mary Magdalene, Joanna, and Susanna helped support Jesus out of their own pockets (Luke 8: 1-3). And the fact that they had something in their pockets probably meant that they were working. Wherever the idea that women shouldn't work came from, it wasn't from the Bible. What would Jesus' ministry have looked like without the support and devotion of the women who participated in his work? And what would our church communities look like today without the work of women? "Women are already working," writes Katelyn, "in the home, outside of it, for their families, for their neighbors, for the glory of God." The Proverbs 31 woman, along with the women who worked with Jesus and Paul, reflect all of those women and all kinds of work.

Think It Through

1. Had you ever heard Proverbs 31? If so, what attributes of the woman were lifted up? How was she presented to you?

2. Before reading this book, did you know that there was a female apostle? How does it feel to realize that Junia was an apostle working alongside Paul? Why do you think churches don't talk about her more often?

3. Katelyn is critical of the phrase "work-life balance." Instead of two "separate spheres," there should be life in work and work in life. What do you think of the quest for "work-life balance"?

4. Katelyn writes, "It's obvious that work can become an idol, a source of ultimate meaning that replaces God. But motherhood can also become an idol—a source of identity and self-worth that will not last." In what ways can both work and motherhood become idols in our world? How do you guard against that in your own life?

5. To what extent does our society provide support for women who work outside the home? Are these resources enough?

6. Some people today might jokingly call the Proverbs 31 woman "supermom." Who gets called names like that in today's world? How is such name-calling harmful to women?

Bring It Home

What do you think it would be like to be among the women who were following and supporting Jesus? What do you imagine their lives were like? Do you think they left their husbands and children behind, or were they independent women? What would daily life have been like as a female disciple of Jesus?

Write It Down

Read the following excerpt from A Woman's Place. Choose one (or both) of the questions and write a response in a journal or notebook.

"Attaching manhood to work and womanhood to the home is a perfect example of well-meaning Christians confusing deeply bound cultural norms for biblical duty. And when such norms are elevated to spiritual prescriptive, so enter unfounded guilt and unfounded judgment. They have kept many women from pursuing work outside the home. And they have kept women from seeing the value of work they do inside of it."

1. Did you grow up with the belief that men were meant to work and women should stay at home? What roles did your parents take on during your childhood? Did you aspire to have a career as a young girl?
2. When you consider family members or friends who choose to stay at home, do you think of them as working? Why or why not?

Pray About It

Dear God, thank you for creating me in your image with willing hands to work. Let my work be fulfilling to me and in the service of others. Thank you for your Scripture and the wealth of models of working women you have provided there. As I labor each day, help me remember their stories and examples. And while I may not be as productive and tireless as the Proverbs 31 woman, let me delight in my own work and remember the legacy of all the working women before me. Amen.

Session 5

YOU ARE FEMALE, AND IT IS GOOD

Session 5

YOU ARE FEMALE, AND IT IS GOOD

Explore the Message

After God created male and female, he surveyed everything he had made and saw that it was "supremely good" (Genesis 1:31). But do we really believe that our femaleness is a gift? Do we celebrate femininity as a core part of who we are and what makes us valuable? Katelyn Beaty says that we should and that the world needs women *as women* in order for our churches and institutions to thrive.

The most important thing about you is that you bear the image of God. Human beings were created male and female not only so we could create more image bearers, but so we could be in relationship with one another. Katelyn compares this concept to the trinitarian God: separate persons who are in relationship and yet totally other. We were created in the image of God to work, to be in relationship with each other, and to be *female*.

Throughout much of history there has been an understood hierarchy with men given superiority over women. Aristotle thought he saw this hierarchy reflected in nature, and later Christian theologians thought they saw it in Scripture: women were seen as inferior to men because Eve didn't obey God in the garden and only considered to bear the image of God when they were with their husbands. Reformation thinkers believed women were inferior and excluded them from public life as punishment for this early transgression. In the eighteenth and nineteenth centuries, women were thought to be weak and in need of protection from the public realm and industrial work. As Katelyn points out, it is clear that these men had never consulted with a woman on what it takes to care for small children!

Thankfully, all Christians today affirm that women are human, and that they bear the image of God just like men do. Yet some Christian communities continue to treat women differently by limiting them to particular roles, like supporter or helper, or identifying them primarily with certain virtues, such as gentleness or peace. Some see all women primarily as nurturers and make that the only feature of their identity, whether they have children or not. But there are plenty of women who are leaders and managers, whether they run companies, preside over courtrooms, manage mutual funds, or run a very tight ship at home. All women—including mothers—have many roles, gifts, and experiences. The spectrum of our possibilities and experiences is wide and not limited by our femaleness.

Katelyn gives the concrete example of Christian conferences, where most of the main speakers are men and women speak on "women's issues" in the periphery. Though women's conferences continue to be popular and draw huge audiences, she questions why women should be relegated to their own conferences. Do we have such vastly different spiritual needs than men? Of course, there are benefits to gathering in Christian community with other women. The point is not to abolish women's conferences, but to encourage more female leadership in other Christian conferences.

Though some Christian communities continue to struggle with the identity and roles of women, it's clear that women were central to the story of Jesus. Think of Mary, the mother of Jesus, whose femaleness was absolutely central to her work in God's story of salvation. Women worked alongside Jesus, they were present at the Crucifixion, and they were the first to find that he was no longer in the tomb. Jesus appreciated women *as women*. And later, when the Apostle Paul wrote that in Christ "there is no longer male and female" (Galatians 3:28 NRSV), the point wasn't to strip human beings of their maleness and femaleness, but to eliminate division and exclusion, affirming that the only requirement for becoming a member in God's family is believing in Jesus.

As we figure out how to bear the image of God in all our spheres of influence, including our professional lives and our home lives, we can remember that being a woman is an important part of this. "Your femaleness is not an accident," Katelyn writes, "it is not a liability. It is a real and good part of who you are, a direct imaging of God." And how we live into and express our femaleness is as varied and diverse as we are as individuals. Some of us are passionate about caring for others. Others of us love solving problems and building things. Femaleness doesn't negate any of these things but enhances all of them. In other words, there's not one way for a woman to live into the image of God. As Katelyn writes, "Your gender is a gift and not an accident, and also not the most important thing about you. Now go figure out what God wants you to do with it."

Read the Scripture

So God created mankind in his own image,
  in the image of God he created them;
  male and female he created them.
  Genesis 1:27 (NIV)

[1]On the day God created humanity, he made them to resemble God [2]and created them male and female. He blessed them and called them humanity on the day they were created.
  Genesis 5:1b-2

There is neither Jew nor Greek; there is neither slave nor free; nor is there male and female, for you are all one in Christ Jesus.
  Galatians 3:28

For we are God's handiwork, created in Christ Jesus to do good works, which God prepared in advance for us to do.
  Ephesians 2:10 (NIV)

Ask the Questions

1. Has your understanding of God's design for humanity changed as you've worked through this study and examined the Creation stories? If so, how?
2. How do you see men and women treated differently in the world around you? How do you feel about these differences? Where do you see the message that men are more important than women, or vice versa? Are there any noticeable differences in the ways your church community values or treats women and men?
3. Katelyn suggests that the most important thing about you is that you bear the image of God, not your gender. Would you agree, and why or why not? What do you think is the most important thing about you?

Apply God's Word

Can you imagine a world with no male and female? Some people think that's what Paul was talking about in Galatians 3:28 when he wrote, "There is neither Jew nor Greek; there is neither slave nor free; nor is there male and female, for you are all one in Christ Jesus." But this verse is not about erasing gender differences. Instead, it's about overcoming barriers or divisions: ethnic ("Jew nor Greek"), social ("slave nor free"), and sexual ("male and female"). In Christ, these distinctions are no longer important; what is important is that all people are made equal and none will hold power over another.

In Paul's vision, the church will be a transformed community. Human beings were created "male and female" (Genesis 1:27), but if the church is to be a new creation, then there must be no gender divisions that oppress. It's not that those who are in Christ will stop being men and women, but that gender is no longer a reason to exclude or dominate. The most prominent feature for any of us is our unity in Christ. Writing about Galatians 3:28, Katelyn explains, "In Christ, gender no longer determines who's in and who's out of the newly formed gospel family.

The idea [of Galatians 3:28]
is unity in contrast to diversity—
the common ground shared
in Christ. Unity or oneness
does not mean uniformity.
Oneness does not mean equal
in an unqualified sense;
it usually connects different
things that have something
in common. In this case, what the
Jew/Gentile, slave/free, and
male/female have in common
is a shared spiritual status
before the Lord. Within God's
household, all are in Christ.[1]

1.   *Women's Evangelical Commentary: New Testament*, ed. Dorothy Kelley Patterson and
      Rhonda Harrington Kelley (Nashville: B&H Publishing Group, 2011), 522.

The only factor for becoming a member of God's family is believing in his Son. And the Son has invited women to himself."

As women, we are all "God's handiwork" (Ephesians 2:10 NIV), created to be female (Genesis 1:27), and so our femaleness is the source of as much value as our very humanity. These beautiful words from the Vatican affirm the intentionality and worth of our female identity: "The sexual differences between man and woman, while certainly manifesting physical attributes, in fact transcend the purely physical and touch the very mystery of the person."[1] In other words, there is no separating you from your female identity. It is part of the exquisite mystery of who you are. In Christ, there is simply no power dynamic between male and female, just as there is no longer any difference between Jew and Greek, slave and free. We are made female in God's original creation, and we remain beautifully and perfectly female in the new creation transformed by Jesus Christ.

Ephesians 2:10 also lifts up the theme of a new creation in Christ. "We [Christians] are God's handiwork [or, God's creation], created in Christ Jesus to do good works" (NIV). There are really two creations going on here: God's original creation, and the new creation in Christ Jesus in which we are created to "do good works." The original Greek here is *ergon*, from the same root as *ergazomai*, which means "to work." So we see that in both stories of creation, human beings are created to work. And in that work, gender no longer matters. As Paul writes in Galatians 6:15, "What matters is a new creation."

What Paul is describing may be a bit like a utopia. After all, today's world still has many obstacles related to being female, and we have all experienced being treated differently because of being a woman. But we can be encouraged by this vision of a transformed world in which male and female are equally beautiful and valuable, and we can know that in Christ, whether today or in the future, we are all one.

---

1.   Michael Sharkey and Thomas Weinandy, eds., "Communion and Stewardship: Human Persons Created in the Image of God" in *International Theological Commission*, vol. 2 Texts and Documents 1986–2007 (San Francisco: Ignatius Press), 330.

Think It Through

1. Have you ever heard the text of Galatians 3:28 preached in your church community? If so, how was it interpreted? If you were to preach about this verse, what message would you hope to communicate?

2. Both the original Creation story (Genesis 1–2) and Paul's "new creation" (Galatians 3:28 and Ephesians 2:10) place an emphasis on work for both sexes. How do you see your own work in light of these verses? In what specific ways does your work participate in God's creation?

3. In Christ, we are all united and equal even though there are differences. How have you seen this unity as you worship with other Christians?

4. In our communities, there are obvious differences of race, social standing, and gender. What should be our attitude toward these differences as Christians? What does it mean to be "in Christ" here and now on the earth?

5. What does it mean to be a family? Read Galatians 3:28 again and add the word "family" after "one": "You are all one family in Christ Jesus." Does that change the meaning of the verse? Why or why not?

6. What adjectives would you use before the word *Christian* to describe your Christian identity (e.g., faithful, loving, American, female)? Think of as many as you can that apply to you. Now imagine life according to Galatians 3:28, when all of those adjectives fall away. What defines you when you are in Christ and all are one?

Bring It Home

Have you ever been treated negatively because you are a woman? What was the situation? What did it feel like? Now think of a time when you were valued *because* of being female. What was that experience like? What is it like to have your gifts valued as a Christian woman living out her faith—in your faith community, your local community, your workplace, your home?

Write It Down

Read the following excerpt from A *Woman's Place*. Choose one (or both) of the questions and write a response in a journal or notebook.

"We have established that we bear the image of a Worker God and are thus called and invited to work, to have dominion over the works of God's hands, as Psalm 8 tells us. What if our femininity is intended not to hinder that call but to enrich it? What if our neighbors and institutions and churches need women *as women* in order to thrive?"

1. How does your femininity enrich your call to work and have dominion over the works of God's hands?
2. What gifts can you contribute to your family, friends, and community especially because of your femininity? How might you celebrate your feminine gifts?

Pray About It

Dear God, thank you that we can be different in amazing ways and yet one in Christ. Today I celebrate the gift of being female, and I give thanks that I am wonderfully made a woman by your loving hands. Help me to use my gifts for my family and my community so I can be the best mother, sister, daughter, and friend that I can be. Enfold me with your love so that I can be a truly beautiful woman to myself and others. Amen.

Session 6

HOW SHE DOES IT ALL

Session 6

HOW SHE DOES IT ALL

Explore the Message

For many of us, motherhood—either the future possibility of motherhood or the reality of it—affects all the other work we might pursue. Even if we are not mothers ourselves, our lives intersect daily with women who are—sisters, friends, neighbors, coworkers. So we know that for some of us, motherhood is at the center of our daily work experience, while for others of us the work of mothering is done in tandem with other good work. In fact, more of us may find ourselves in the latter category according to recent findings that indicate 71 percent of all American mothers are engaged in paid work.[1]

Whether or not you're a mother, you've probably encountered the ongoing cultural debate in one way or another: Can women really "have it all"? That is, can we pursue challenging and rewarding careers while also raising children and having a strong marriage? The reality for those of us who are mothers and work outside the home is that often we come home to a "second shift" of housework and domestic demands.

---

1.   "Stay-at-Home and Working Mothers, 1970 and 2012," Pew Research Center (April 7, 2014), http://www.pewsocialtrends.org/2014/04/08/after-decades-of-decline-a-rise-in -stay-at-home-mothers/sdt-2014-04_moms-at-home-0-03/.

A major 2014 survey by the Barna Group found that 62 percent of Christian moms are dissatisfied with their work/life balance, and 34 percent feel that their church community doesn't provide much social or emotional support for them.[1] Katelyn identifies three main barriers for those of us wanting to pursue a meaningful professional life and an invested family life at the same time: bodies, bosses, and what she calls the "official bureau of lady judgment."

With regard to bodies, only we women can carry children, and there is a limited period of time in which we can do so. Pregnancy, birth, postpartum experience, and breastfeeding all can take a serious toll on our bodies and can place limitations on our work in ways that new fathers do not face. Even if we do not bear our children in our own bodies, the physical demands of mothering are great. Many of us have experienced the deep bond between mother and child that also can complicate a return to work. As beautiful and rewarding as it is, the reality is that a woman's physical experience of having children—of being a mother—can make the balance of work and family life more complicated.

The second barrier Katelyn identifies is bosses, which brings us to the subject of family leave. Did you know that only 12 percent of U.S. employees in the private sector are guaranteed access to paid family leave?[2] In fact, of 170 developed countries, only two don't mandate financial assistance to women during maternity leave: the U.S. and Papua New Guinea. Although policies have improved in the U.S., still it is clear that our culture does not support working mothers as it should. Some companies have no family leave policy at all, forcing some women to choose between having children and having a job. Perhaps you or someone you know has been in a similar situation, struggling to overcome the barrier of a workplace that is not "family friendly."

Finally, what Katelyn calls the "official bureau of lady judgment" reveals a third obstacle we can face when trying to have both career and family: other women. The so-called "Mommy Wars" rage on, with some

---

1   "Tired & Stressed, but Satisfied: Moms Juggle Kids, Career & Identity," Barna Group (May 5, 2014), https://www.barna.com/research/tired-stressed-but-satisfied-moms-juggle-kids-career-identity/

2.   "DOL Factsheet: Paid Family and Medical Leave," United States Department of Labor, (June 2015), https://www.dol.gov/wb/resources/paid_leave_fact_sheet.pdf

of us issuing subtle and not-so-subtle judgments about one another's parenting styles and family choices. Judgments of stay-at-home mothers and working mothers come packaged in passive-aggressive statements about the boredom of staying home or the difficulty of being away from children every day. And with all the research and information out there about parenting styles and techniques, there are endless critiques about attachment parenting, breastfeeding, vaccinations, and many other issues. Have you ever heard mothers discussing these issues and falling into criticism of each other?

What is the solution to this tangle of obstacles? Katelyn offers three ideas. First, we can exchange the phrase "work/life balance," which pits home and work against each other, for "work/home integration," which allows both work and home to belong to the family. It feels far more doable to integrate home and work than it does to balance two huge things like work and life! Next, our faith communities can help husbands to better understand and embrace the Christian vision for marriage and fatherhood, which centers on the call to love one's neighbor—and in fact, the closest neighbors are the wife and family. The selflessness of neighbor love should be the basis for our relationships and division of work in the family. Finally, it is crucial for husbands to support our callings outside the home if that's what we choose to pursue. Katelyn writes, "Despite its messiness, the new marriage model is also an invitation: for husbands and wives to pursue a family vocation—to craft a culture of industry, interdependency, and love, all for their children to thrive."

Toward this end, our Christian communities must raise the bar for fathers. Dads who participate in routine care of children are not babysitters; they are parents. And as Christians, we all are responsible for advocating a pro-family agenda that values both motherhood and fatherhood in the workplace as well as the home. In all discussions of family, Katelyn suggests, there should be "buckets and buckets of grace" for working moms and stay-at-home moms alike. With regard to mothers criticizing or pressuring other mothers, she writes, "On matters about which Scripture is silent, it is best to extend to each other freedom rather than create new rules for holiness." Those of us who pursue some activity outside the home—a job, a hobby, something we love—often credit our outside pursuits with making us better mothers.

God's forgiveness, and knowing that we are forgiven sinners, frees us from the very things that spoil our relations with each other. It frees Christian mothers from the need to prove anything. It frees us from envy and one-up-mothering. It frees us from the craving for approval and praise that we seek from others. It liberates us to value each other in Christ, and to love our mother-neighbors as ourselves.[1]

---

1.   Gloria Furman, "Mommy Wars in the Local Church: A Parable," Desiring God, May 24, 2012, http://www.desiringgod.org/articles/mommy-wars-in-the-local-church-a-parable.

Read the Scripture

⁵May the God of endurance and encouragement give you the same attitude toward each other, similar to Christ Jesus' attitude. ⁶That way you can glorify the God and Father of our Lord Jesus Christ together with one voice.

⁷So welcome each other, in the same way that Christ also welcomed you, for God's glory.

Romans 15:5-7

⁹Jesus told this parable to certain people who had convinced themselves that they were righteous and who looked on everyone else with disgust: ¹⁰"Two people went up to the temple to pray. One was a Pharisee and the other a tax collector. ¹¹The Pharisee stood and prayed about himself with these words, 'God, I thank you that I'm not like everyone else—crooks, evildoers, adulterers—or even like this tax collector. ¹²I fast twice a week. I give a tenth of everything I receive.' ¹³But the tax collector stood at a distance. He wouldn't even lift his eyes to look toward heaven. Rather, he struck his chest and said, 'God, show mercy to me, a sinner.' ¹⁴I tell you, this person went down to his home justified rather than the Pharisee. All who lift themselves up will be brought low, and those who make themselves low will be lifted up."

Luke 18:9-14

Ask the Questions

1. Do you think women really can "have it all"? Why or why not? What does that phrase mean to you? What do you think are the primary challenges for women who have children and also work outside the home (or work from home)?
2. How does your church community show support or consideration for mothers who work outside the home? How have you (or women you know) been encouraged as you seek to integrate work and home life?

3. Have you ever encountered or witnessed the "official bureau of lady judgment"? If so, how have you heard women criticize other women related to work and family choices, including how they raise their children?

Apply God's Word

Passive-aggressive commentary like that of the "official bureau of lady judgment" is alive and well in the parable of the Pharisee and the tax collector. In his prayer, the Pharisee castigates the tax collector and sings his own praises. He gives thanks that he is not like the tax collector—whose sins we can only imagine—and congratulates himself for fasting and tithing. It is certain that the tax collector can hear this prayer even though he is standing off to the side. The Pharisee certainly sounds like a morally upright human being, and the tax collector has only a desperate plea for mercy to offer. But at the end of the parable, Jesus switches things up. It is the humble tax collector who leaves the temple justified rather than the righteous Pharisee.

While the Pharisee considers himself to be a pretty big deal where religion is concerned, he's actually missing the entire point, which is humility. In a similar way, when we criticize each other for working outside the home or staying at home, we miss the point. Have you ever heard a stay-at-home mother say, "I just couldn't be away from my children every day"? Or have you heard a mom who works outside the home say, "I just know I would get bored if I were at home all day," or perhaps, "I'd love to be able to stay home, but we all don't have that luxury"? What's missing in comments such as these is humility—and encouragement. Why are some mothers so polarized simply because of different choices?

In Romans 15:5-7, Paul prays for his listeners to have "endurance and encouragement," to worship God "with one voice," and to "welcome each other." This is also the message of the parable. Had the Pharisee been as religious as he thought he was, he would have turned to the tax collector with a spirit of welcome and encouragement. As Christian women—whether or not we're mothers ourselves—we would do well to declare a cease-fire in the Mommy Wars and find ways to lift each other up and encourage each other. Passive-aggressive comments, whether they come in the form of a tax collector's prayer or a mom's insecure remark, do little to live into the Romans 15:5-7 call for welcome.

Surely, our humility need not take the form of falling to the floor and crying out for mercy. But remember that our Christian piety doesn't need to criticize and judge others for their choices. Working outside the home, staying at home, family beds, attachment parenting, organic food, time-outs—these are choices for parents to make, not grounds for critical comments or ending friendships. There are endless opportunities for us to encourage each other as mothers and "glorify the God and Father of our Lord Jesus Christ together with one voice," as Paul counsels us to do.

Think It Through

1. What has been your experience or observation of the "Mommy Wars"? Do you have friends or family members who have strong opinions about whether a mother should stay at home or work outside the home?

2. The parable of the Pharisee and the tax collector teaches a message of repentance and humility. How does your insight into the parable's message change when you imagine two mothers praying side-by-side?

3. Romans 15:5-7 prays that we will adopt an attitude of encouragement and welcome. How can you be more encouraging and welcoming in your own interactions with mothers? In what ways can you affirm the choices of mothers you know?

4. Katelyn points out that the United States is one of only two developed countries that does not provide paid maternity leave. What do you think of that fact? How do you think Christians should respond, and why?

5. Katelyn writes, "Every woman I met who worked outside the home while raising young children said that she could do neither well without her husband's *full support of her calling.*"

What does it mean for a husband to fully support his wife's calling? What are the different ways that might play out? How can single mothers find the support they need to live out their calling and responsibilities?

6. What could your church community do to support mothers who work outside the home, affirm mothers who choose to stay at home, and help families with "work/home integration"?

Bring It Home

When you were growing up, did your mother work outside the home, stay at home, or perhaps do both in different seasons? How did you feel about her choice(s)? How did your church community support your mother and other mothers who made different choices? If you can, ask your mother how she felt about her choice. Would she change anything now? Why or why not?

Write It Down

Read the following excerpt from A *Woman's Place*. Choose one (or both) of the questions and write a response in a journal or notebook.

"Perhaps more than anything, what today's moms need is grace. Grace to endure the evolving nap schedules and temper tantrums and moralistic mommy blogs and sheer exhaustion. Grace to make the right decisions for a child, even when those decisions are different from a peer's. Grace to know that God sees and delights in a mother's love for her children, in all the ways that love could be expressed."

1. If you have children, what are your greatest needs as a mother? How do you respond to Katelyn's words on grace? If you don't have children, consider the experience of a mother who is close to you. What kind of grace do you think she needs?

2. What do you think Katelyn means by "grace" in the passage above? How would you define that term in the context of your own experience or observation of motherhood?

Pray About It

My God, you have called some of us to be mothers and all of us to be mothering. Thank you for the blessing of children. Let us seek one another in friendship rather than judgment and encourage each other as we work to raise or influence the children in our lives. Give us strength to be compassionate and caring as we enjoy the company of other mothers and respect their choices. Amen.

Session 7
A FRUITFUL LIFE

Session 7

A FRUITFUL LIFE

Explore the Message

Have you ever seen your family tree? Think about its gentle web of branches and names extending one from the other. How do you envision your own place on that tree? It may seem that the way to take a meaningful place among the branches is to marry and have children. But is that the only way to live a meaningful Christian life? As women, we often face the assumption from family, church, and society that we will marry and have children and that this will make us complete. But according to Katelyn Beaty, this is not the only way to have a fruitful Christian life, and Scripture bears out this truth.

A positive theology of work for women allows us to be fruitful in more ways than one. Katelyn writes, "Fruitfulness is simply all the ways that our God-given resources—time and energy and bodies and brains and relationships—are invested in order to bear seeds of shalom in and for God's world." In other words, we can be fruitful in all kinds of ways: in our work, in our friendships, in our creative pursuits. In Scripture, fruitfulness extends beyond having children. Katelyn is a single woman in her thirties—what can fruitfulness mean for her, and for other unmarried women? Being single in a church community is challenging when the activities and worship services assume an audience of married parents. And when you were in college, did you sometimes feel that there was an assumption that your primary goal was to get married?

Christian history is replete with single women on mission for Jesus Christ. Women such as Lydia, Phoebe, and Junia were commended by Paul for their work for the gospel, not their marital status or ability to have children. Virgin martyrs lived and died for Christ in the second and third centuries, and professional religious women in the Middle Ages lived in community and did important work separate from men. Women in subsequent years have moved into many other spheres of ministry.

For Katelyn, hope for marriage was hard to let go of. After a broken engagement and a promotion at work, she realized that her aspirations for marriage had less to do with the relationship she had been in and more to do with the idea that marriage and children would provide her with a secure identity—an idea that many of us share and receive from our culture as we grow up. "Marriage is a real and good desire, and it remains one of my own," she writes. "But it is neither the capstone of maturity nor the scope of God's purposes for his followers." Did you ever feel that marriage was inevitable, or even necessary, for you to have a fulfilled life? Fortunately, there are many ways for us to live into God's will, and marriage is only one of them.

Scripture offers hope, not condemnation, for those of us who will not marry or have children. While children are usually seen as a blessing in the Old Testament, in some places eunuchs and barren women are celebrated (Isaiah 54; 56). Jesus' ministry contradicts the idea that marriage and family are essential to living out God's promises. The most important marriage becomes the one between Christ and his church (Ephesians 5:22-33), and the main family is made up of the followers of Christ. Jesus even scolded those who would make their own biological family more important than the family of believers (Matthew 19:29; Mark 10:29; Luke 14:26). The branches of this tree stretch and grow regardless of marriage and children. You can be sure that there is a flourishing family that you belong to whether your future includes marriage and children or a fruitful single life.

Read the Scripture

⁴⁶While Jesus was speaking to the crowds, his mother and brothers stood outside trying to speak with him. ⁴⁷Someone said to him, "Look, your mother and brothers are outside wanting to speak with you."

⁴⁸Jesus replied, "Who is my mother? Who are my brothers?" ⁴⁹He stretched out his hand toward his disciples and said, "Look, here are my mother and my brothers. ⁵⁰Whoever does the will of my Father who is in heaven is my brother, sister, and mother."

Matthew 12:46-50

⁷I wish all people were like me, but each has a particular gift from God: one has this gift, and another has that one.

⁸I'm telling those who are single and widows that it's good for them to stay single like me....

³²I want you to be free from concerns. A man who isn't married is concerned about the Lord's concerns—how he can please the Lord. ³³But a married man is concerned about the world's concerns—how he can please his wife. ³⁴His attention is divided. A woman who isn't married or who is a virgin is concerned about the Lord's concerns so that she can be dedicated to God in both body and spirit. But a married woman is concerned about the world's concerns—how she can please her husband. ³⁵I'm saying this for your own advantage. It's not to restrict you but rather to promote effective and consistent service to the Lord without distraction.

1 Corinthians 7:7-8, 32-35

¹Sing, barren woman who has borne no child;
    break forth into singing and cry out,
        you who were never in labor,
    for the children of the wife who has been deserted will be more numerous than the children of the married, says the LORD.

²*Enlarge the site of your tent,*

    and stretch out the drapes of your dwellings;

    don't hold back.

    Lengthen your tent ropes and strengthen your stakes.

    ³*To the right and to the left you will burst out,*

    and your children will possess the nations' land

    and settle their desolate cities.

Isaiah 54:1-3

⁴*The* LORD *says:*

    To the eunuchs who keep my sabbaths,

    choose what I desire,

    and remain loyal to my covenant.

    ⁵*In my temple and courts, I will give them*

    a monument and a name better than sons and daughters.

    I will give to them an enduring name

    that won't be removed.

Isaiah 56:4-5

Ask the Questions

1. When you were young, did you dream of growing up to get married and have children? Or did you imagine yourself as a single person making her own way in the world? What kind of cues did you receive from your church and family?
2. Think of the single people you know, or if you are single, reflect on your own experience. In what ways can the single life be fruitful? How does your church community reach out to single Christians?
3. Some of us choose not to have children, but others struggle with infertility. Read again the above Scriptures from Isaiah. How might these comfort someone in this situation? What would you say to a Christian friend who wonders how her life can be fruitful without the gift of children she so desperately wants?

Jesus' recurring message appears to be that the traditional commitments of marriage, home, and family never provide legitimate grounds for not responding to the call of discipleship. The ultimate bond of the *new family* through the gospel is even stronger than that of one's physical earthly family.[1]

We are all called to minister to each other and the world around us. Single Christians play a valuable role within that mission, but their role cannot be fully realized unless they have the support of the rest of the church body.[2]

1. Barry Danylak, *Redeeming Singleness: How the Storyline of Scripture Affirms the Single Life* (Wheaton, IL: Crossway, 2010), 168.

2. Christine A. Colón and Bonnie E. Field, *Singled Out: Why Celibacy Must Be Reinvented in Today's Church* (Grand Rapids, MI: Brazos Press, 2009), 17.

Apply God's Word

The advent of Jesus and his ministry brings with it new ideas about marriage and family. There are some surprising reversals: those who remain single are celebrated, and Jesus' followers are instructed to abandon their biological families. But while single Christians today might struggle with how to live a fruitful life as a single person, the fruit of the single life is celebrated in the New Testament. Without the distractions of marriage, Paul wrote, single Christians had more time to focus on the gospel (1 Corinthians 7:32-35). "Service to the Lord" (1 Corinthians 7:35) and "the Lord's concerns" (1 Corinthians 7:34) should be primary according to Paul, and the necessary obligations of marriage (1 Corinthians 7:32-35) lead to one's attention being divided between the marriage and the work of the Lord.

Paul didn't forbid or advise against marriage; he only pointed out that those of us who are not married are in a better position to do the work of the gospel because we are not distracted. Married persons must be aware that their concerns are divided and be careful to attend to both the work of the marriage and the work of God. Paul was like a good manager giving instructions to his retail staff: If you are married, be sure that you can still provide "effective and consistent service to the Lord without distraction" (1 Corinthians 7:35).

For Paul, being single is one gift among the many possible gifts. He wishes everyone could be single like him, but each has "a particular gift from God" (1 Corinthians 7:7). He advises those who are single to remain single. The objective he has in mind is clear: single people are free to dedicate themselves to God's work, as he does. But what about the command to "be fruitful and multiply" (Genesis 1:28 NRSV)? Single followers of Christ were fruitful in their work as they multiplied the community of believers. In the new life in Christ, many ideas about marriage and family were simply turned on their heads.

Jesus envisioned a new family of disciples that replaced the biological family. For those of us who are unmarried and/or are without children, this offers hope for a family tree that extends in spite of our singleness. "Jesus' very life and ministry challenge the notion that marriage and family are the primary stage for God's promises and purposes," Katelyn writes. "Jesus regularly used familial language for his followers and rebuked those who would place loyalty to family above loyalty to him...all of our family trees will someday reach an end. But there is another tree whose branches stretch on and on." Being in the family of Jesus provides an enduring family tree, one that grows regardless of marriage or children. Yet Jesus' language about family is sometimes harsh: "Whoever comes to me and doesn't hate father and mother, spouse and children, and brothers and sisters—yes, even one's own life—cannot be my disciple" (Luke 14:26). But the point is clear: he has come to establish a new family of believers, and if you want to be a part of that, you have to be all in.

God's promises in the Old Testament also contain the flavor of reversal. The Book of Isaiah twice praises those who have no children and promises a legacy for them. The barren woman in Isaiah 54 will have more children than anyone (v. 1), and the faithful eunuchs in Isaiah 56 will receive "a monument and a name / better than sons and daughters" (v. 5). This speaks both to those who are unable to have children and those who choose not to (as many eunuchs become sterile as a matter of choice). In the Gospel of Matthew, we see eunuchs who have "made themselves eunuchs because of the kingdom of heaven" (19:12) This is the ultimate expression of Paul's later advice to remain single. To these single-by-choice eunuchs, Jesus says, "Those who can accept it should accept it" (19:12).

The Bible contains a number of places for single Christians to find inclusion and embrace. Paul welcomed single women into his ministry (such as Lydia, Phoebe, and Junia), and Jesus established a family of believers that created new extended-family relationships for everyone who followed him. Remember that Jesus himself was single, and his life was perhaps the most fruitful in the history of the world. There are many ways to live a fruitful life in Christ, and marriage and children are only part of the story.

Think It Through

1. What did Jesus mean when he commanded his followers to abandon their biological families in order to be part of the

community of believers? How are we to apply that Scripture today?

2. Do Christians put too much emphasis on marriage as a key to fulfillment and happiness? Do you think marriage has become an idol for many of us? Why or why not?

3. When Paul cautions married persons to be careful of distractions from the word of God, he also suggests that single people are in a better position to do the work of the gospel. How might relationships be distracting from your relationship with Christ? How might they actually enhance that relationship?

4. Paul writes that he wishes all people could be single. Why do you think Paul advocated singleness? In what ways can singleness be a gift?

5. When you think of Christians who have devoted themselves to a celibate life (such as nuns or religious sisters), what do you think their singleness means to them? How are their lives fruitful?

6. Is having a family the only way to live into God's command to "be fruitful and multiply" (Genesis 1:28 NRSV)? What are other ways to fulfill that instruction that don't include marriage or children?

Bring It Home

For those who are married: When you were single, how did you think about marriage? Did you embrace your singleness? Did you value the extra time and energy you had to devote to your work in Christ? What do you miss today about being single?

For those who are single: How do you think about marriage? Do you embrace your singleness? Do you find that you have extra time and energy to devote to your work in Christ? If you get married, what will you miss about being single?

Write It Down

Read the following excerpt from A *Woman's Place*. Choose one (or both) of the questions and write a response in a journal or notebook.

"In Christ...I am not left barren and bereft, I am not forgotten to history, because in him there is a family tree I belong to, whose branches are anyone who calls on his name in faith. In him my life bears fruit, and in the coming kingdom, in its upside-down way, more are the children of the desolate woman than of her who has a husband (Isaiah 54)."

1. How would you describe what it means to be fruitful in Christ?
2. What does it mean for the "desolate woman" to have more children than the woman who has a husband? How does this Scripture from Isaiah relate to Jesus' words on family?

Pray About It

Dear God, I give thanks to you that I may have a fruitful life in your Son whether I am single or married. Even if marriage and children are in the distant future for me, you will now and always be my very near present. As we live according to your calling, we all can find our family among other believers and together flourish in faith. Let us find comfort in your word knowing that regardless of our marital status, the branches of our family tree will grow and prosper in the community of faith. Amen.

Session 8

EMBRACING AMBITION

Session 8

EMBRACING AMBITION

Explore the Message

What do you think when you hear the word *ambition*? Ambition is a concept that is often seen negatively because it is so focused on the self. There are many examples of ambition gone wrong in our popular culture, people letting their aspirations take over their good judgment and good will for others. Katelyn Beaty considers ambition in light of Scripture: "Ambition is defined as humans striving to be like God apart from the power of God." Ambition has gotten a bad rap among early theologians, but Katelyn argues that ambition was always part of what God intended for us. He doesn't want us *not* to have ambition; he wants us to use it for good.

Consider this: the most ambitious person who ever lived is Jesus. He was single-minded in his will with just one desire: "doing the will of the one who sent me and … completing his work" (John 4:34). He wanted to preach the gospel, heal the sick, raise the dead, and take up the cross toward his most important work. This is the kind of ambition that we should have as followers of Christ. Katelyn writes, "Oriented toward God, *ambition is the setting of the will to accomplish the desire of the heart.*"

It is pushing toward shalom, living as the *tsaddiqim*, or taking the risk of going on mission for Christ. It's a virtue, but a difficult one for us to claim.

Ambition is not always viewed positively when it comes to our identity as women. Our culture seems to say that either we can be loving and nurturing or we can be ambitious, but we can't be both. It's a stark contrast. But the question should be more nuanced than that: what kind of ambition are we talking about? Is it God-directed? Are we seeking to accomplish God's will and purposes? Ambition can be very good when it's the kind of ambition that Jesus had, or the expression of a pure desire of a woman's heart to be on mission for Christ. Being ambitious does not negate or distract from being a devoted Christian, an ethical woman, or a faithful wife and mother.

Mainstream culture often applies a traditional version of ambition to us women, assuming that if we have ambition then we aspire to climb a corporate ladder or master a business enterprise. Of course many of us *do* have goals in the business world, but that's not the only place that our ambition can take root. Ambition in our culture is often about material gain. Christian culture sometimes juxtaposes contentment and ambition, as though we cannot be content and ambitious at the same time. But discontent is natural, and human beings were created to be ambitious, to govern the works of God's hands and to master all the living creatures. However, godly ambition always faces real human limitations, and part of living in Christ is embracing our limits.

We all face the limits of our embodied lives. We are finite human beings, we are mortal, and we can only do one thing at a time. However, these limits don't have to quell our ambitions; rather they can help us know what desires are the most important by guiding us away from some goals and toward others. Even God had limits when he took on the human body of Jesus. Through him, God worked within the limits we all face every day. God knows our limits. Katelyn writes, "The ambition God invites us to is a cross-shaped ambition: to embrace our inability to have it all so that he may be our all." We must keep our ambitions and remember who equips us to fulfill his will. We should always know whom those ambitions serve, who calls us to work, and who calls us to reign.

Read the Scripture

Jesus said to them, "I am fed by doing the will of the one who sent me and by completing his work."

John 4:34

Instead, desire first and foremost God's kingdom and God's righteousness, and all these things will be given to you as well.

Matthew 6:33

¹All people on the earth had one language and the same words. ²When they traveled east, they found a valley in the land of Shinar and settled there. ³They said to each other, "Come, let's make bricks and bake them hard." They used bricks for stones and asphalt for mortar. ⁴They said, "Come, let's build for ourselves a city and a tower with its top in the sky, and let's make a name for ourselves so that we won't be dispersed over all the earth."

⁵Then the LORD came down to see the city and the tower that the humans built. ⁶And the LORD said, "There is now one people and they all have one language. This is what they have begun to do, and now all that they plan to do will be possible for them. ⁷Come, let's go down and mix up their language there so they won't understand each other's language." ⁸Then the LORD dispersed them from there over all of the earth, and they stopped building the city. ⁹Therefore, it is named Babel, because there the LORD mixed up the language of all the earth; and from there the LORD dispersed them over all the earth.

Genesis 11:1-9

³⁵James and John, Zebedee's sons, came to Jesus and said, "Teacher, we want you to do for us whatever we ask."

³⁶"What do you want me to do for you?" he asked.

³⁷They said, "Allow one of us to sit on your right and the other on your left when you enter your glory."

³⁸Jesus replied, "You don't know what you're asking! Can you drink the cup I drink or receive the baptism I receive?"

³⁹"We can," they answered.

Jesus said, "You will drink the cup I drink and receive the baptism I receive, ⁴⁰but to sit at my right or left hand isn't mine to give. It belongs to those for whom it has been prepared."

⁴¹Now when the other ten disciples heard about this, they became angry with James and John. ⁴²Jesus called them over and said, "You know that the ones who are considered the rulers by the Gentiles show off their authority over them and their high-ranking officials order them around. ⁴³But that's not the way it will be with you. Whoever wants to be great among you will be your servant. ⁴⁴Whoever wants to be first among you will be the slave of all, ⁴⁵for the Human One didn't come to be served but rather to serve and to give his life to liberate many people."

Mark 10:35-45

Ask the Questions

1. What are your first thoughts when you hear about a woman who is "ambitious"? What about when you hear about an ambitious man?
2. Have you ever thought of Jesus as ambitious? What are some of the ways he displays ambition in the Gospels? Jesus is not ambitious in the way that our culture defines that word. How would you define the kind of ambition Jesus displays?
3. When you were growing up, were you encouraged to be ambitious, or encouraged to achieve your goals? Or did you ever experience someone telling you not to be ambitious? What were your aspirations when you were a child? Did anyone encourage you to follow those dreams?

Apply God's Word

What do you think about the story of the tower of Babel? The people had a great ambition to build a city and a tower to reach all the way up to the sky. They could strive to accomplish this because they all spoke one language and could understand one another and collaborate.

It is always painful to compare our motives with Christ's. It is not wrong for believers to be industrious or ambitious, but when ambition pushes obedience and service to one side, it becomes sin. Pride or insecurity can cause us to overvalue position and prestige. In God's kingdom, such motives are destructive. The only safe ambition is for Christ's kingdom, not our own advancement.[1]

---

1.   *The Handbook of Bible Application: Second Edition*, ed. Neil S. Wilson (Wheaton, IL: Tyndale House Publishers, 2000), 29.

When God saw what they were planning, he didn't like their ungodly ambition or their tower reaching up to the sky. He made it so they all spoke different languages and couldn't communicate. Now the dream of the tower of Babel would never be fulfilled.

The lesson of the tower seems to be that ambition can be misplaced or reach too far, in this case, too high up in the sky. God did not look kindly on that kind of ambition because its motives were selfish and prideful. Jesus, too, had his limits with ambition that was out of control. When James and John wanted to sit at his side, Jesus told them those places are already reserved. And when the other disciples bickered with James and John for even asking such a question, Jesus told them all that aspiring to be first and greatest would make them servants and slaves. It seems that ambition had no place in Jesus' ministry.

But then Jesus announced his own ambition: "to serve and to give [my] life to liberate many people" (Mark 10:45). So maybe it's not ambition *per se* that causes problems, but only the self-serving kind. Trying to build a tower to the sky to reach God is the wrong kind of ambition because it elevates the people rather than God, and brings them glory rather than giving glory to God. It is prideful. Scrambling to sit right beside Jesus is the wrong kind of ambition. But doing God's will of serving and liberating many people is ambition of another sort. Ambition, then, is defined by what it's aiming for.

Have you ever felt shamed for being a woman with ambition? Many people think that ambition is the sole province of men, but it doesn't always look so good on them, as we see with James and John. Ambition belongs to everyone, and God means for everyone to have it—even women, even *Jesus*. It's the kind of ambition that matters. Jesus makes it clear: "desire first and foremost God's kingdom and God's righteousness, and all these things will be given to you as well" (Matthew 6:33). As long as God's kingdom and righteousness are first in your mind, your ambitions will take you in the right direction.

Think It Through

1. Why do you think God was so angry about the tower of Babel? What kind of ambition did the people display in their desire to build a tower to the sky?

2. As women, we are sometimes shamed for being ambitious. Have you ever felt shamed for being a woman with ambition? If so, when? "She's very ambitious" is rarely a compliment. Why do you think that is? How does Scripture affirm our God-given ambitions?

3. How can the obstacles and human limitations we face help us clarify our ambitions? How does Jesus model those human limits for us?

4. Katelyn writes, "The ambition God invites us to is a cross-shaped ambition." What do you think she means by that? How would you define or explain "cross-shaped ambition"?

5. How does the story of James and John clamoring to sit beside Jesus resonate in your own life? Have there been times when you have tried to be the first or the greatest? What happened in those instances? What did you learn?

6. Paul wrote, "I make it my ambition to proclaim the good news" (Romans 15:20 NRSV). What kind of ambition did he have? What were the outcomes of this ambition?

Bring It Home

What are your ambitions today? How do you determine if these ambitions, your heart's desires, are in line with God's will? What are the next steps that would move you toward what God intends for your life?

Write It Down

Read the following excerpt from A *Woman's Place*. Choose one (or both) of the questions and write a response in a journal or notebook.

"Rather than dismissing ambition outright, we need to ask what ends our ambitions serve and amplify those ambitions when they serve good, holy ends."

1. When you consider your own ambitions, do you find their ends to be good and holy? How can engaging in spiritual disciplines such as prayer, reading Scripture, or talking to a trusted friend help you evaluate your ambitions?

2. It is necessary for ambition to have ends that are good and holy, but what about the means of achieving them? As you work to reach your aspirations, are you following a course that is God-directed?

Pray About It

Dear God, Infuse my heart with healthy ambition. Help me to remember that my greatest ambition is the gospel so that I may model Jesus' goal to do your will and complete your work on earth. I want the desire of my heart to be to do your will and live into the life you intend for me. My ultimate worth comes from knowing and loving you, not from my personal accomplishments. Thank you for your grace and patience as I aspire to live into your will. Amen.